SECOND EDITION

English Across the Curriculum

Content-area Vocabulary and Skills

3

Margaret Martin Maggs

National Textbook Company
a division of *NTC Publishing Group* • Lincolnwood, Illinois USA

1996 Printing

Table of Contents

Dictionary Definitions

How do you read the dictionary?

The dictionary tells us the definition of a word, what a word means. Sometimes a word has more than one meaning. Here is an example:

> **play** v. 1. to move lightly 2. to sport or frolic 3. to operate repeatedly 4. to take part in a game 5. to perform on a musical instrument 6. to act on the stage

Sometimes a word can be used in a sentence in different ways. The word **play**, for example, can be used as a noun and as a verb. The definitions for the verb are listed together, and the definitions for the noun are listed together. Here is the word **tie**, for example. **V** means verb and **n** means noun:

> **tie** v. 1. to draw together, to fasten by a cord or other bond 2. to make a loop or knot 3. to equal in score 4. to restrict or limit   n. 1. something used to draw together 2. a plank or rod used to hold parts together 3. something tied 4. a restriction 5. a common interest 6. equality of numbers

It is important to understand that a word can have more than one definition. When you look for the meaning of a word, try that meaning in a sentence to be sure that you have the correct one.

Here are some sentences with the word **tie** in them. After the sentence is the number of the correct meaning:

> I **tied** the book on my bicycle. (v. 1)   The game was a **tie**. (n. 6)   That is a railroad **tie**. (n. 2)   My family has **ties** with another country. (n. 5)

How do you read the dictionary?

A Write the number of the correct definition for <u>fall</u>
beside each sentence.

> **fall** v. 1. to drop from a higher to a lower place   2. to be dropped or spoken   3. to
> extend downward   4. to be taken captive   5. to die   6. to diminish   n. 1. the act of
> dropping   2. something which has dropped   3. autumn

1. She asked, "Did you <u>fall</u> downstairs?" _____ *(Definition v. 1)* _____

2. The <u>fall</u> is my favorite time of year. _____

3. The <u>fall</u> of leaves is beautiful. _____

4. The capital city <u>fell</u> to the enemy. _____

5. How long did the rain <u>fall</u>? _____

B Find the word <u>tear</u> in a dictionary. It has several
definitions. Copy the definition that goes with each
sentence.

1. A <u>tear</u> fell from her eyes. <u>Tear</u> in this sentence means

_____

2. Can you <u>tear</u> the paper in two? <u>Tear</u> in this sentence means

_____

3. There is a <u>tear</u> in that girl's dress. <u>Tear</u> in this sentence means

_____

C Find the word <u>bow</u> in the dictionary. It has several
different definitions. Copy the definition that goes with
each sentence.

1. The musician used a <u>bow</u> on his violin. <u>Bow</u> in this sentence means

_____

2. What a pretty <u>bow</u> on that package! <u>Bow</u> in this sentence means

_____

3. After the show, the singer <u>bowed</u> to his fans. <u>Bow</u> means

_____

More about the Dictionary

How do you read the dictionary?

The dictionary presents the definitions of words. Sometimes it gives us other information, too. Some dictionaries have synonyms of words. Synonyms are words with the same meanings.

<u>little</u>	is a synonym of	<u>small</u>
<u>right</u>	is a synonym of	<u>correct</u>

Some dictionaries have antonyms. Antonyms are words that have opposite meanings.

<u>big</u>	is an antonym of	<u>little</u>
<u>wrong</u>	is an antonym of	<u>right</u>

Some definitions have other forms of the word. Verbs are an example of this. The word **fell** is another form of the word **fall**.

fall (p. and p.p. **fell**)

Or, you may see an example like this:

pliable adj. 1. flexible 2. easily influenced. adv. pliably n. pliability n. pliableness

This definition has three words similar to <u>pliable</u> in it: <u>pliably</u>, <u>pliability</u>, <u>pliableness</u>.

Here is a complete definition with synonyms, antonyms and related words:

tear (p. **tore**, p.p. **torn**) v. 1. to pull apart 2. to scratch or lacerate n. a rent, a hole Syn. v. rip, split, cleave (See **break**) Ant. v. mend, weld, reunite, join

How do you read the dictionary?

A Find the word happy and its synonyms in a dictionary. Copy each sentence below and change the word happy to a synonym. Use a different synonym for each sentence.

1. He was happy to see her.

_____

2. My family is happy in our new house.

_____

3. My birthday is usually a happy day.

_____

B Find the word like and its synonyms in a dictionary. Copy each sentence below and change the word like to a synonym. Use a different synonym for each sentence.

1. I really liked your father.

_____

2. Tom likes Mary.

_____

3. The building was very tall and wide, like a mountain.

_____

C Find these words in the dictionary and copy the similar words in their definitions:

1. fly: _____

2. light: _____

3. come: _____

How do you read the dictionary?

The dictionary gives us the definitions of words. It also shows us how to pronounce them. At the beginning of most dictionaries, you will find a page that has a special chart called the pronunciation key. The pronunciation key gives symbols for different sounds. After each of these symbols, there is an example word or words to show the sound. To help you even more, on the right-hand page in most dictionaries, you will find a smaller pronunciation key that repeats the information.

Here is part of a pronunciation key with example words:

a	bat, sat	i	sit, is	oi	boy, oil
ā	ate, late	ī	ice, my	ou	how, out
ä	jar, far	o	top, stop	ə	cup, about
e	met, get	ō	open, coat	u̇	put, look
ē	equal, easy	ô	order, more	ü	rule, food
ėr	term, bird				

Try pronouncing each sound. You can use this key to pronounce sun (sən). Look for the sound ə in the chart. Say the sample words—cup and about. Now you know that the u in sun is pronounced like the u in cup and the a in about.

How do you read the dictionary?

A Find the example words from the pronunciation key for each word below. Copy them on the lines beside the dictionary pronunciations.

1. sun   (sən)   _____
2. pave   (pāv)   _____
3. endorse (endôrs)   _____
4. appoint (əpoint)   _____
5. dip   (dip)   _____
6. year   (yir)   _____
7. tribe   (trīb)   _____
8. precede (prēsēd)   _____
9. moor   (môr)   _____
10. under   (əndėr)   _____
11. luck   (lək)   _____
12. condor (kondôr)   _____
13. moth   (môth)   _____
14. music   (müzik)   _____
15. team   (tēm)   _____
16. show   (shō)   _____
17. father (fäthėr)   _____
18. link   (lēnk)   _____
19. tool   (tül)   _____
20. take   (tāk)   _____

a	bat, sat
ā	ate, late
ä	jar, far
e	met, get
ē	equal, easy
ėr	term, bird
i	sit, is
ī	ice, my
o	top, stop
ō	open, coat
ô	order, more
oi	boy, oil
ou	how, out
ə	cup, about
ù	put, look
ü	rule, food

Accents

How do you read the dictionary?

When we pronounce a word, we must know the sounds of the letters in the word. We must also know which part is stressed or pronounced more loudly. That part has the accent. The dictionary helps us learn the accents of words.

Some dictionaries use this sign ' to show which part of the word has the accent. The words look like this:

de • ny'   In this word the accent is on the second part or syllable.

sub'• ject   In this word the accent is on the first part or syllable.

af • ter • noon'   In this word the accent is on the third part or syllable.

Some dictionaries use capital letters for the syllable that is accented. The words look like this:

A • gent   In this word the accent is on the first syllable.

par • TIC • u • lar   In this word the accent is on the second syllable.

pa • RADE   In this word the accent is also on the second syllable.

When you look in the dictionary for the pronunciation of a word, be sure to see which syllable has the accent.

How do you read the dictionary?

A   Which syllable has the accent? Write 1, 2, or 3.

1. advantage   ad VAN tage   _2_   7. umbrella   um BREL la   _____

2. reason   REA son   _____   8. puzzle   puz'zle   _____

3. telegraph   tel'e graph   _____   9. mistake   mis TAKE   _____

4. frozen   fro'zen   _____   10. thunderstorm   thun'der storm _____

5. wherever   wher ev'er   _____   11. different   DIF fer ent   _____

6. generous   GEN er ous   _____   12. envelope   en'vel ope   _____

B   Look for these words in the dictionary. Copy them with
their accents. Put the number of the accented syllable
beside the copied word.

1. department   _____ *de part' ment*   2 _____

2. welcome   _____

3. gasoline   _____

4. property   _____

5. Saturday   _____

6. telephone   _____

7. October   _____

8. delightful   _____

9. painting   _____

10. giraffe   _____

Putting Facts Together

What is a category?

When you are learning facts it can help to put the facts together in groups. These groups are called categories. Some books do this for you, but sometimes you have to do it yourself.

Here is an example of some categories in a history book:

Qualifications for Senators
Age: 30 years or over
Citizenship: Must have been a citizen for at least 9 years
Residence: Must reside in the state he or she represents

Qualifications for Members of the House of Representatives
Age: 25 years or over
Citizenship: Must have been a citizen for at least 7 years
Residence: Must reside in the state he or she represents

Sometimes you must decide on the categories. One of the usual ways to put things together in a category is when they are examples, like this:

man, neighbor, girl, teacher   are   examples of people
secretary, nurse, doctor, lawyer   are   examples of jobs

Another way to put facts together in a category is when they are reasons, like this:

eating incorrectly, not sleeping enough and bad health habits
are
reasons for becoming ill

What is a category?

A Put the words in one of the three categories. You can use a word more than one time:

woman   umpire
football eggs
team   milk
boy   soccer
candy   referee
player   cake

SPORTS	FOOD	PEOPLE
_____	_____	_____
_____	_____	_____
_____	_____	_____
_____	_____	_____
_____	_____	_____

B Write the missing word on the line:

1. chair, desk, table, television   are examples of _____

2. buying food, paying rent, buying clothes   are reasons for _____

3. September, week, Tuesday, afternoon   are examples of _____

4. red, white, yellow, blue   are examples of _____

5. going to movies, watching television, listening to records   are examples of _____

6. better pay, nicer people, good working conditions   are reasons for _____

7. hamburgers, french fries, pizza   are examples of _____

8. fever, headache, broken leg   are reasons for _____

9. chicken, rice, eggs   are examples of _____

10. mailing a letter, sending a package, buying a stamp   are reasons for _____

MISSING WORDS: fast food   times   earning money   colors
going to the doctor   supermarket food   changing jobs
going to the post office   entertainment   furniture

Putting Ideas Together

How can you put ideas together?

You can put facts together in categories. You can put ideas together in categories, too. Putting ideas into categories sometimes helps you understand them better.

One way to put ideas together is to make categories of

> where
> when
> how

Here are some examples:

over and under	tell	where
easy and difficult	tell	how
tomorrow and today	tell	when

Knowing categories can help you study for tests. When you group the facts or the ideas together, you will find them easier to understand.

Knowing categories can help you memorize. When you have many facts or ideas to remember, you will find them easier to learn when you put them together in categories.

Remember these basic categories:

> reasons
> examples
> where
> when
> how
> who

How can you put ideas together?

A Write the missing category on the line. Use <u>where</u>,
<u>when</u>, <u>how</u>.

1. loud and soft   tell   _____*how*_____

2. now and then   tell   _____

3. here and there   tell   _____

4. up and down   tell   _____

5. someday and sometime   tell   _____

6. good and bad   tell   _____

7. inside and outside   tell   _____

8. clean and dirty   tell   _____

9. always and never   tell   _____

10. east and west   tell   _____

B Which word does not belong with the others? Write it
on the line.

1. man, boy, box, girl   _____*box*_____

2. thing, thank, talk, take   _____

3. middle, center, love, side   _____

4. tall, short, run, fat   _____

5. you, me, Lester, her   _____

6. Nick, Sally, John, teacher   _____

7. read, talk, listen, white   _____

8. composition, report, sing, book   _____

9. fever, cold, pain, doctor   _____

10. September, May, Tuesday, January   _____

How can you use words better?

In any language, you do not often use one word by itself. You use words in groups. When you understand the relationships or connections between words, you will use them better. An analogy is a relationship or connection between words or phrases. This is an analogy:

<u>mother</u> is to <u>daughter</u> as <u>father</u> is to <u>son</u>

Many times you will see an analogy written with symbols. These are the symbols:

:   means   is to
:: means   as

or

mother : daughter :: father : son

Many tests have analogy problems on them. One way to understand an analogy is to look for synonyms. Synonyms are words that mean the same.

<u>funny</u> means the same as <u>amusing</u>
<u>happy</u> means the same as <u>glad</u>
<u>funny</u> : <u>amusing</u> :: <u>happy</u> : <u>glad</u>
(<u>funny</u> is to <u>amusing</u> as <u>happy</u> is to <u>glad</u>)

Here are more synonyms:

book — volume   report — composition
correct — right   incorrect — wrong
talk — speak   hear — listen

and their analogies:

book : volume :: report : composition
correct : right :: incorrect : wrong
talk : speak :: hear : listen

How can you use words better?

A Write the letter of the synonym on the line.

1. little   a) big   b) small   c) good   _____

2. home   a) house   b) office   c) bedroom   _____

3. dinner   a) breakfast   b) meal   c) cook   _____

4. pleased   a) thank   b) fine   c) happy   _____

5. see   a) listen   b) speak   c) look   _____

6. synonym   a) same   b) different   c) word   _____

7. car   a) cat   b) automobile   c) bus   _____

8. meat   a) leave   b) buy   c) beef   _____

9. leave   a) tree   b) go   c) come   _____

10. bad   a) good   b) wrong   c) right   _____

11. dozen   a) eggs   b) loaf   c) twelve   _____

B Complete the analogy. Write the letter of the correct synonym on the line.

1. study : learn :: evening : _____   a) light   b) night   c) right   _____

2. night : evening :: helper : _____   a) assistant   b) worker   c) teacher   _____

3. deposit : put in :: withdraw : _____   a) borrow   b) save   c) take out   _____

4. one : first :: two : _____   a) second   b) third   c) number   _____

5. writer : author :: father : _____   a) son   b) papa   c) child   _____

6. true : right :: false : _____   a) correct   b) good   c) wrong   _____

7. know : learn :: country : _____   a) city   b) nation   c) world   _____

8. read : study :: plus : _____   a) and   b) minus   c) easy   _____

9. large : big :: good : _____   a) delicious   b) nasty   c) easy   _____

10. build : make :: ask : _____   a) answer   b) example   c) question   _____

Understanding Relationships–Numbers

How can you use numbers better?

When you understand the relationships between words you can use the words better. When you understand the relationships between numbers you can do better in Math. There are analogies in Math, too. Here is one:

$$1 : 1 :: 2 : 2$$

Analogies are not always synonyms. Here is another number analogy:

$$3 : 6 :: 4 : 8$$

In this analogy 3 + the same number (3) = 6, and 4 + the same number (4) = 8. What is the same is the relationship between 3 and 6 and 4 and 8. It is the same relationship as:

$$4 : 8 :: 10 : 20 \quad \text{or} \quad 3 : 6 :: 7 : 14$$

Look at this number analogy:

$$1 : 3 :: 7 : 9$$

In this analogy 1 + 2 = 3 and 7 + 2 = 9. This is the same relationship as:

$$7 : 9 :: 10 : 12 \quad \text{or} \quad 1 : 3 :: 8 : 10$$

Here is another number analogy:

$$1 : 3 :: 7 : 21$$

Here you have $1 \times 3 = 3$ and $7 \times 3 = 21$
Here is a number analogy with division:

$$10 : 5 :: 18 : 9 \quad (10 \text{ divided by } 2 = 5 \text{ and } 18 \text{ divided by } 2 = 9)$$

Doing number analogies can be fun and can help you see the relationships between numbers.

How can you use numbers better?

A Write the letter of the correct number to complete the number analogy on the line.

1. 3 : 6 :: 8 : ____	a) 16	b) 10	c) 4	_____
2. 7 : 10 :: 5 : ____	a) 7	b) 8	c) 9	_____
3. 10 : 15 :: 15 : ____	a) 10	b) 18	c) 20	_____
4. 24 : 20 :: 16 : ____	a) 12	b) 20	c) 10	_____
5. 8 : 15 :: 20 : ____	a) 25	b) 27	c) 30	_____
6. 9 : 2 :: 13 : ____	a) 6	b) 2	c) 9	_____
7. 46 : 30 :: 100 : ____	a) 90	b) 84	c) 75	_____
8. 28 : 56 :: 1 : ____	a) 4	b) 8	c) 2	_____
9. 11 : 0 :: 12 : ____	a) 2	b) 0	c) 3	_____
10. 31 : 48 :: 15 : ____	a) 32	b) 46	c) 79	_____

B Write the letter of the correct number to complete the number analogy on the line.

1. 3 : 9 :: 8 : ____	a) 24	b) 16	c) 8	_____
2. 20 : 4 :: 25 : ____	a) 9	b) 5	c) 10	_____
3. 1 : 10 :: 5 : ____	a) 18	b) 15	c) 50	_____
4. 18 : 3 :: 36 : ____	a) 6	b) 12	c) 9	_____
5. 16 : 4 :: 40 : ____	a) 16	b) 20	c) 10	_____
6. 8 : 64 :: 7 : ____	a) 49	b) 35	c) 63	_____
7. 5 : 1 :: 8 : ____	a) 2	b) 1	c) 4	_____
8. 12 : 36 :: 4 : ____	a) 12	b) 8	c) 1	_____
9. 1 : 2 :: 2 : ____	a) 3	b) 4	c) 5	_____
10. 10 : 2 :: 50 : ____	a) 10	b) 5	c) 15	_____

How can you use words better?

Analogies, as you know, are relationships. Some word analogies are synonyms, words that mean the same thing. Other word analogies are antonyms, words that mean the opposite thing.

These are antonyms:

good	is the antonym of	bad
soft	is the antonym of	hard
warm	is the antonym of	cool

Many tests have analogy problems using antonyms. Here are more antonyms in analogies:

open : close :: good : bad
right : wrong :: soft : hard
frown : smile :: cry : laugh
absent : present :: useless : useful

Some analogy tests have both antonyms missing. These tests and their correct answers can look like this:

frown : ____ :: cry : ____
a) smile — frown   b) smile — laugh   c) soft — hard   __B__

useless : ____ :: absent : ____
a) right — wrong   b) useful — present   c) open — close   __C__

How can you use words better?

A Write the letter of the antonym on the line.

1. little   a) big   b) small   c) good   _____

2. antonym   a) same   b) synonym   c) word   _____

3. breakfast   a) meal   b) dinner   c) food   _____

4. early   a) clock   b) time   c) late   _____

5. happy   a) sad   b) pleased   c) glad   _____

6. noisy   a) quiet   b) shout   c) study   _____

7. correct   a) good   b) right   c) wrong   _____

8. up   a) above   b) down   c) over   _____

9. often   a) never   b) daily   c) sometimes   _____

10. dirty   a) bad   b) nasty   c) clean   _____

11. old   a) young   b) slow   c) more   _____

B Complete the analogy. Write the letter of the correct antonym on the line.

1. first : last :: top : _____   a) side   b) bottom   c) box   _____

2. more : less :: plus : _____   a) add   b) minus   c) multiply   _____

3. strong : weak :: wide : _____   a) narrow   b) small   c) big   _____

4. before : after :: first : _____   a) last   b) now   c) later   _____

5. early : late :: hot : _____   a) warm   b) on time   c) cold   _____

6. long : short :: tall : _____   a) short   b) big   c) long   _____

7. north : south :: left : _____   a) east   b) right   c) west   _____

8. yell : whisper :: fake : _____   a) real   b) false   c) right   _____

9. loud : soft :: black : _____   a) white   b) brown   c) red   _____

10. rich : poor :: ill : _____   a) sick   b) cold   c) well   _____

Understanding Relationships–
Part to Whole

How can you use words better?

You can use words better when you understand their relationships or analogies. Some word analogies are synonyms or antonyms. Some word analogies are related because they relate words for a part to words for a whole.

A foot is part of a leg. A hand is part of an arm.

The analogy is

foot : leg :: hand : arm

Here are some more analogies of part to whole:

A student is part of a class. A player is part of a team.
student : class :: player : team

A room is part of a house. An office is part of a building.
room : house :: office : building

A show is part of what you see on television. A play is part of what you see
in a theater.
show : television :: play : theater

Some analogy tests have the part missing like this:

_____ : day :: day : month   a) month   b) hour   c) night   _**B**_

Some analogy tests have the whole missing like this:

water : _____ :: page : book   a) wet   b) bridge   c) ocean   _**C**_

How can you use words better?

A Here are words for parts. Find the whole and write the letter on the line.

1. light	a) sun	b) dark	c) window	_____
2. son	a) father	b) family	c) mother	_____
3. word	a) language	b) see	c) class	_____
4. eye	a) mouth	b) ear	c) face	_____
5. food	a) eat	b) meal	c) drink	_____
6. teacher	a) school	b) student	c) room	_____
7. bed	a) sleep	b) bathroom	c) bedroom	_____
8. October	a) spring	b) year	c) month	_____
9. brake	a) car	b) tire	c) garage	_____
10. foot	a) arm	b) face	c) person	_____

B Complete the analogy. Write the letter of the correct letter on the line.

1. airplane : airport :: ambulance : ____	a) car	b) hospital	c) nurse	_____
2. clerk: store :: secretary : ____	a) office	b) executive	c) good	_____
3. month : year :: minute : ____	a) month	b) hour	c) watch	_____
4. desk : office :: machine : ____	a) appliance	b) building	c) factory	_____
5. afternoon : day :: dessert : ____	a) dinner	b) sweet	c) coffee	_____
6. letter : post office :: tooth : ____	a) dentist	b) mouth	c) teeth	_____
7. city : country :: country : ____	a) world	b) city	c) vacation	_____
8. fan : stadium :: executive : ____	a) lawyer	b) secretary	c) office	_____
9. book : library :: room : ____	a) bath	b) kitchen	c) house	_____
10. mother : family :: father : ____	a) family	b) work	c) son	_____
11. Tuesday : week :: hour : ____	a) morning	b) right	c) day	_____

How do you put facts together?

When you learn words, you learn what they mean. When you put one word with another word, you can have other meanings. For example, you know these words:

tall   that   boy

When you put those words together you have a new meaning:

that tall boy

When you put one sentence with another sentence you can have a new meaning, also.

Apples are fruit.
I like fruit.

MEANS

I like apples.

You can do this with several sentences:

It was very dark and quiet. I was all alone among the trees. I couldn't see the path. Suddenly I heard a strange sound.

MEANS

I was in the forest at night.

"Don't you like my dinner?" asked Eliza. Tom looked at his plate. He didn't want Eliza to feel bad. "I'm not very hungry," he said.

MEANS

Tom doesn't like Eliza's dinner.

How do you put facts together?

A Choose the meaning. Write the letter of the correct meaning on the line.

1. He gets 100 on every test.   MEANS   a) He is my friend.   b) He is a good student.   c) He is a student in my class. _____

2. My mother went to sleep watching television.   MEANS   a) It was not a good show.   b) She is old.   c) She was tired. _____

3. Jack asked to borrow my library card.   MEANS   a) The library is close to my house.   b) He needed a book.   c) He reads well. _____

4. She took a taxi to work.   MEANS   a) She has a job.   b) It was raining.   c) She is an executive. _____

5. Wasn't it bad when Lisa was late?   MEANS   a) Lisa isn't nice. b) She didn't come on time.   c) Being late is bad. _____

B Choose the correct meaning of each paragraph and write the letter on the line.

1. "What's your sister's telephone number?" asked Franco. "Why do you want it?" Chu said. "I thought I'd call her up. There's a good movie playing downtown," Franco answered.
a) Chu has a sister.   b) Franco wants to go out with Chu's sister.   c) Franco goes to the movies every night. _____

2. First we heard the sound. Then we could see it, a silver bird in the sky. Soon we were saying hello to my grandmother.
a) Planes look like birds.   b) We went to the airport yesterday.   c) My grandmother came on a plane to visit us. _____

3. You must know Sonia. Your sister is her friend and always talks about the many brothers and sisters she has.
a) Sonia's part of a large family.   b) Sonia's a student.
c) Sonia's a good friend. _____

Facts That Mean the Same

How do you put facts together?

When you read words or write them, you can often use different words to mean the same thing. For example,

> You are my friend.

means the same thing as

> I like you.

Here is another example:

> The cat asked for his dinner.

means the same thing as

> The cat wanted some food.

Or

> The dress was red and white like her shoes.

means the same thing as

> She wore red and white shoes to match her dress.

Or

> The old man walked slowly up the stairs.

means the same thing as

> When he climbed the stairs, you could see that he was old.

It is important to remember that you can use different words to say the same facts. Think about this when you read. Think about this when you write. It will help you to read better and write better in English.

How do you put facts together?

A Match the sentences that mean the same thing. Write the letter of the sentence from Column 1 beside the sentence from Column 2 that is the same.

COLUMN 1:
A. That was a good show.
B. I waited a long time for them.
C. Milton started the car and left.
D. "Thank you for my gift," she wrote.
E. My uncle showed us his garden and his chickens.
F. Please turn off that television set and listen to my problem.
G. She wasn't very nice to me.

COLUMN 2:
1. He drove away. _____

2. It was very entertaining. _____

3. He lives in the country. _____

4. They were late. _____

5. Someone sent her a present. _____

6. I don't like her. _____

7. I need help. _____

B When the sentences mean the same thing, write S on the line. When they mean something different, write D on the line.

1. I love to go to the stadium to see a game.
   I am a fan. _____

2. She worked hard and saved her money.
   She wanted a new washing machine. _____

3. "Where were you last night?" asked my mother.
   I wasn't home yesterday evening. _____

4. He put the key in the door, opened it and called to the children, "Here's Daddy."
   The father is going into his home. _____

5. There were many patients waiting.
   The emergency room was full of people. _____

What Sentence Will Come Next?

How do you think ahead?

You can learn to write more clearly. You can better understand what you read also. One way to do this is to think ahead. When you write or when you read, think about the next sentence. What will it say? What do you expect it to say?

Here is a sentence:

The road up the mountain was very long, but I didn't care.

What do you think will be the next sentence? It could be

I wanted to see the view from the top of the mountain.

When you think ahead, you are helping yourself to understand better what you are reading or what you want to write.

Here is a group of sentences. What do you think will be next?

"Won't you come in and sit down?" said Andrew. "I'm happy to see you. Did you want to talk to me about something?"

The next sentence will probably say what the visitor wants to talk about. Here is another example:

My mother is a lawyer. She works very hard.

What do you think will be the next sentence? It will probably tell what kind of work she does as a lawyer.

You will not always be correct when you think about what comes next. Sometimes there are several possible things that might come next. It will help you, though, to think ahead, and most of the time you will be right. This thinking ahead is called predicting.

How do you think ahead?

A Read each group of sentences. Decide which sentence will be next and write an X next to it.

1. The old woman looked out the window and said, "What a beautiful day." Her daughter said, "Yes, spring is here."

_____ a) "Would you like to go outside and sit in the sun?"

_____ b) "Would you like to read a book?"

_____ c) "Would you like to clean the bedroom for me?"

2. The pilot walked through the airplane saying hello to the passengers. A little boy of 4 said to him, "I want to be a pilot when I'm older."

_____ a) The pilot answered, "You're too young, son."

_____ b) The pilot answered, "I hope you are, son."

_____ c) The pilot didn't answer him.

3. The little cat was soft and cute. "Oh, Mommy, he's so sweet," said Susie. "Please let me keep him."

_____ a) Her mother said, "You're sweet, Susie."

_____ b) Her mother said, "Go to school, Susie."

_____ c) Her mother said, "Will you be responsible for him, Susie?"

4. Every Saturday I help my father at his store. "I want you to learn about working," he says to me. "Life isn't all play, you know."

_____ a) I answer, "You're wrong, Dad."

_____ b) I answer, "It's Saturday, Dad."

_____ c) I don't answer him.

What Happens Next?

How do you think ahead?

When you read or write it always helps to think about the next sentence. It helps even more when you think about what happens in the next several sentences. The more you can think ahead or predict, the better you will read or write.

Here is an example:

> They went to a dance club after dinner. "What a wonderful place," Angie said. "I'm so glad we came here. I love to dance."

What is going to happen next? They are going to dance, of course, and they will probably dance for a long time because Angie enjoys it so much. This information may not be in one sentence. It could be in two or three sentences, but you should be able to expect it.

What do you think will happen next after this?

> The nurse said, "Please sit down. I'm afraid you will have to wait for the doctor. He's very busy now. He will tell you how ill your friend is as soon as possible." The students from Nick's class looked at each other. What could be the matter?

If you are thinking ahead, you will probably be able to predict that the doctor will see Nick's friends a little later and tell them why Nick is sick.

Remember, the more you can predict what will happen next, the better a reader and writer you will be.

How do you think ahead?

A Read each paragraph. Decide which prediction is true and write an X on the line next to it.

1. "This is our biggest match of the year," said the soccer coach. "We've been practicing hard all week, and I know you're ready."
   _____ a) Next the coach will say that the other team is better.
   _____ b) Next the coach will tell the team to play their best.
   _____ c) Next the coach will tell the players that soccer is dangerous.

2. The announcer said, "Mr. K Jeans are the best you can buy. The styling is perfect for every size of man, woman and child. And now you can buy them in all the spring colors."

   _____ a) Next the announcer will say the price and where to buy them.

   _____ b) Next the announcer will talk about the news.

   _____ c) Next the announcer will say, "Good-bye."

3. Science is my favorite subject. Some people think it is difficult. You do have to study hard. There is a lot to learn.

   _____ a) Next the speaker will say why Science is a favorite subject.

   _____ b) Next the speaker will talk about Social Studies.

   _____ c) Next the speaker will say how to study.

4. I like reading tall tales. One of my favorite characters is the giant lumberjack Paul Bunyan. In one tale, he knocked down a mile of trees rolling over in his sleep!
   _____ a) Next the speaker will tell more about Paul Bunyan.
   _____ b) Next the speaker will talk about mystery stories.
   _____ c) Next the speaker will talk about trees.

Predicting the End

How do you think ahead?

Predicting what happens next can help you read and write better. The more you can predict the better you will understand and organize information. When you can predict what will happen at the end of a story or composition you are reading or writing, you will be a better student.

It is easier to predict the end of a composition you must write or information you must read for school. Usually the end of your composition or the chapter of your school book will be a summary.

For example:

In Nancy's Social Studies textbook Chapter Seven begins:

> "There are many reasons for the Civil War, or the War Between the States. Some of these reasons were social, but many were economic."

Nancy knows that Chapter Seven will give details about the reasons for the war. The end of the chapter will probably list the reasons in a few short sentences of summary.

Here is another example:

Lon Hai must write a composition on the differences between life in his country and life in the United States. He begins with:

> "Before last January I had never seen or eaten an apple pie, my favorite American dessert. My favorite food then was Dim Sum."

Lon Hai will continue his composition with other examples of differences between his country and the States. He will end with a summary of the main differences.

How do you think ahead?

Finish the predictions below:

1. Nanita is reading a book about famous people. Chapter
Five begins:

> "Martin Luther King was one of the most important
> people in the United States during the Fifties and Sixties.
> He was so famous for his work that he was awarded the
> Nobel Peace Prize. People all over the world were sad
> when he was killed."

Nanita knows that the chapter will continue to talk
about the many things that Martin Luther King did. It

will probably end: _____.

2. Claude is reading a newspaper story. It begins:

> "Do you like to wash windows? John Hustin does. He
> washes windows as a job. He even likes to wash them on
> his vacation."

Claude knows that the story will continue by telling
which windows and where John Hustin washed them. It

will probably end: _____.

3. Ari is writing a composition for his English class on why
people should speak two languages. He begins:

> "I am bilingual because I speak two languages."

Ari will continue by telling what good can come from
knowing more than one language. He will probably end

his composition with: _____.

4.   The television show began with a funny song and dance.
"This is the kind of homework I like," thought Trude.
"Now where are those questions?

Trude will continue watching the show. After it ends

she will probably _____.

Predicting the End

How do you think ahead?

Sometimes it is easy to predict the end of a composition or information that you read. The end is often a summary. It is not as easy to predict the end of a story. You may not be able to predict the exact end, but you can probably make a close prediction or guess about the end of the story.

When you read a detective story, for example, you may not know who the criminal is. You do know, however, that the detective will probably find the criminal at the end of the story.

When you read a story about two people in love, you may not be able to say what exactly will happen at the end. You do know, though, that the two people will probably still be in love at the end.

What do you think will probably happen at the end of this story?

He could hear two men talking outside the window. "Ssh," said one. "Don't wake anybody up or they'll call the police." The other man said, "Who's talking, man? I think you want the police to catch us." Billy lay in bed and thought about what he could do.

What do you think will probably happen? Probably at the end of this story the police will be thanking Billy for helping them catch the two men. If you predicted that, you are ready to practice more predictions.

How do you think ahead?

Finish the predictions for each story.

1. "Oh, I'm sorry," said the smiling girl. "I didn't see you because I had so many packages. Did I hurt you?" Will smiled, "Not at all. You do have a lot of packages. Are you going to the post office with them?" "Yes," she said, "I love my family, but there are so many of them at Christmas time."

This story will probably end with Will and the girl _____

_____.

2. The two boys watched from behind a tree. The silver thing was not a bird. It wasn't a plane, either, although it flew as fast as one. After it landed, everything was very quiet. "Wow! There's a door opening up," Jimmy said. "I'm afraid," answered his friend.

This story will probably end with Jimmy and his friend _____

_____.

3. The doctor called up his lawyer. "Listen," he said. "My patient is very angry. I want you to give me some advice."

This story will probably end with the doctor _____

_____.

4. "I don't care who you are," Jane said to the young man. "Just look at what you did. I worked hard to finish those letters, and now they're all dirty. My boss will be very angry." The young man smiled. "I really am the president of the company," he said. "I'll talk to your boss—and you too—after work, if I can."

This story will probably end with Jane and the president _____

_____.

Deciding on the Facts

What can you believe?

When you read or write, you must know the difference between fact and opinion. This is a fact:

>   My mother's name is Luisa.

This is an opinion:

>   My mother's name is pretty.

A sentence that tells what the speaker feels or thinks is opinion.

Can you tell which sentence is fact and which sentence is opinion?

>   She bought a blue dress.
>   The blue dress looked nice on her.

The second sentence tells an opinion. The first one is fact.

Decide which sentence is fact and which is opinion in these examples:

>   We ate ice cream for dessert.
>   It was the best ice cream in the world!

Again, the second sentence is opinion.

Here are several sentences. Only one is opinion. Can you find it?

>   That pen was made in my father's factory.
>   His pencil was longer than mine.
>   People have a lot of problems, but I don't.

The third sentence is opinion.

What can you believe?

A   Decide which sentences are facts. Write <u>fact</u> on the line next to those sentences.

1. John is nicer than Jerry.   _____

2. I went to school this morning.   _____

3. The Fanas came to this country from Colombia.   _____

4. You are taller than I am.   _____

5. Mr. Lang is an electrician.   _____

6. Ms. Sanchez is an excellent math teacher.   _____

7. Rover is the name of my friend's dog.   _____

8. This is a beautiful painting.   _____

9. I know some English.   _____

10. My grandfather's farm is in California.   _____

B   Decide which sentences are opinions. Write <u>opinion</u> on the line next to those sentences.

1. Basketball is the most exciting sport.   _____

2. She said, "Good morning."   _____

3. Doctors say that cigarette smoking is not healthy.   _____

4. Our class took a trip to the museum.   _____

5. I think that my father is a good dentist.   _____

6. We were singing a song on the bus.   _____

7. The flowers in my native country are beautiful.   _____

8. David said that he was sorry.   _____

9. She is the best friend in the world.   _____

10. Carmen's parties are always fun.   _____

Deciding on the Facts

What can you believe?

You can decide what is fact and what is opinion in many ways. One way is to look for words like THINK or FEEL. You will find words like that in sentences that are opinions. Here are some examples:

> He thinks that she is a good teacher.
> I feel angry about the election.
> I think spring is the nicest time of the year.

Another way to decide when a sentence is opinion is to look for word groups like HE SAYS or THEY SAY or I BELIEVE. Here are some examples:

> Mr. Angelou says that many people are lazy.
> The newspaper says that unemployment is high.
> I don't believe that Tiny is a baseball player.

Another way to decide when a sentence is opinion is to ask yourself questions about it. Ask yourself: Can this be proven? Can this be true for everyone or everything all the time? Here is an example:

> The commercial said **Mr. K Jeans** are the best.

Can **Mr. K Jeans** be best for everyone? Are there any other jeans that are as good as **Mr. K Jeans**? Because an advertisement says something, is it true? The answer to the first and third questions is no. The answer to the second question is yes. That sentence is an opinion.

What can you believe?

Here is a composition. Each sentence is numbered. Read the composition. Decide what each sentence is, Fact or Opinion. Some sentences can include both facts and opinions. Explain why.

MY NEW HOME

1. The United States of America is my new home. **2.** It is a big country, and I only live in one small part of it. **3.** I live at 38 Reardon Avenue. **4.** I like my apartment, and it is my home. **5.** But I also think of all the United States as my home. **6.** Wise people say, "Home is where the heart is." **7.** My heart is with the United States, and that country is my home.

Is Sentence 1 Fact or Opinion? _____

Why? _____

Is Sentence 2 Fact or Opinion? _____

Why? _____

Is Sentence 3 Fact or Opinion? _____

Why? _____

Is Sentence 4 Fact or Opinion? _____

Why? _____

Is Sentence 5 Fact or Opinion? _____

Why? _____

Is Sentence 6 Fact or Opinion? _____

Why? _____

Is Sentence 7 Fact or Opinion? _____

Why? _____

Why and What

What are the cause and the effect?

When you read, you should understand 1) what happened, 2) why it happened, and 3) what the result was. When you write a composition, your reader should understand the same three things. This is called CAUSE (why) and EFFECT (what resulted). Here are some examples:

> Mr. Jones ate breakfast quickly because he was late for work.
> "He was late for work" tells us why (CAUSE)
> "Mr. Jones ate breakfast quickly" (EFFECT)

In many sentences the EFFECT comes before the CAUSE. Many times this keeps people from understanding which is EFFECT and which is CAUSE. Sometimes it helps to change the sentence in your mind. Begin the sentence with "because" like this:

> Because he was late for work, Mr. Jones ate breakfast quickly.

Remember when you write that it is helpful to give the EFFECT in the same sentence as the CAUSE. This is the correct way:

> Because she was tall, Joyce could see easily in a crowd.

It is not correct to have only the CAUSE:

> Because she was tall.

Learn to look for the WHY and the WHAT or the CAUSE and the EFFECT in every sentence with "because." Learn to write the WHAT or EFFECT in every sentence you begin with <u>because</u>.

What are the cause and the effect?

A Finish the sentences below by adding a word to complete the CAUSE.

1. Primo put on his coat because he was _____.

2. Because it was _____, the stores were not open.

3. She took off her shoes because her feet _____.

4. I didn't see you because there were so many _____.

5. Because the class was _____, some people had no seats.

6. We were late because there weren't any _____.

7. Because he was _____, he fell asleep watching television.

8. Because Jane _____, she broke her leg.

9. The fans were happy because their team was _____.

10. John took the job because he needed _____.

B Put each group of sentences together to make one sentence. Use the word "because" to help you.

1. We were late getting home today. There were many cars on the road.

_____

2. The player hit a home run. The fans stood up and cheered.

_____

3. Franz loves Ilse. He asked her to marry him.

_____

4. The weather was getting colder. The birds flew South.

_____

5. We bought chicken. The beef was too expensive.

_____

What and Why

What are the cause and the effect?

Part of writing or reading well is to think well. When we understand the relationship of <u>what</u> happened (EFFECT) and <u>why</u> it happened (CAUSE), we are thinking well. When we don't understand, we don't think well.

Rajid is writing a composition on a famous guitar player. He writes:

> Many people bought tickets to the show because they wanted to hear him play.

Rajid helps us understand the CAUSE (they wanted to hear him play) for the EFFECT (many people bought tickets to the show).

Nuhad is writing a composition, too. This composition is about a famous painter. Nuhad writes:

> Many people went to the museum. The artist and his paintings were famous.

The composition would be better if Nuhad would write:

> Many people went to the museum because the artist and his paintings were famous.

Remember, when you want to begin a sentence with "because," you must always tell what happened (EFFECT). Not:

> Because he was tired.

BUT

> Because he was tired, he went to sleep at ten o'clock.

What are the cause and the effect?

A The sentences are not complete. Some are missing
CAUSE (C). Some are missing EFFECT (E). Write C
or E for the part that is missing.

1. Because the airplane landed on time. _____

2. So they lived happily in their little house. _____

3. And he received an "A" in English. _____

4. Because she was my friend. _____

5. Because they were in love. _____

6. So Jack went home. _____

7. And the candidate was elected. _____

8. Because it was his birthday. _____

9. So we bought a bird. _____

10. Because the class was too big. _____

B These sentences are not complete. Finish them with a
CAUSE or EFFECT.

1. Because the apartment house was burning,

_____.

2. The class president called a meeting

_____.

3. She called me at home yesterday

_____.

4. Because there was a long line at the post office,

_____.

5. Everyone was talking at the same time

_____.

6. We had a good time

_____.

7. I opened a savings account

_____.

Understanding the Meaning

What does it really mean?

When you read, you learn there are many ways to say the same thing. When you write, you can practice what you have learned. Sometimes you can understand a meaning only when you think about all the words together. For example, when you read the following sentence, you understand one fact.

> The bird in the tree sang, "Twee. Twee."

When you read this next sentence, you understand another fact.

> All around the bird was the sweet smell of newly opened flowers.

When you put both sentences together like this:

> The bird in the tree sang, "Twee. Twee." All around the bird was the sweet smell of newly opened flowers.

Both sentences tell you that it is the special time of the year when birds sing and flowers open. The sentences do not use the word "spring," but that is really what the writer is describing.

When you read or write, always remember that when you put words together, you can understand new ideas.

> "I don't like what you did," said her mother. Then she put her arms around her daughter and kissed her.

The writer is showing that the mother didn't like her daughter's actions, but that she still loved her.

Always think about what you are reading or writing to understand the true meaning behind the words.

What does it really mean?

Choose the meaning of the sentences. Write an <u>X</u> next to the correct meaning.

1. It is easy to be a world-famous singer. All you need to do is to study hard, be talented and have good luck. It helps to start early, also, when you are two or three years old.

   This paragraph really says:

   _____ a) That it is easy to be a world-famous singer.

   _____ b) That it is not easy to be a world-famous singer.

   _____ c) That it helps to sing when you can.

2. We stopped the man and asked where the Londons' house was. He said, "First you go three miles on this road. Then you turn right. No, that's not it. Well, you take the next left turn and—no, that won't do it." He stopped and smiled. "I guess the truth is, you can't get there from here."

   This paragraph really says:

   _____ a) That the Londons' house is easy to find.

   _____ b) That the Londons' house is hard to find.

   _____ c) That the man doesn't know where the Londons' house is.

3. "You really are something," his sister said. "Everyone in this family works hard. But you're too good for a job. It's more important that you go out with your friends and then sleep late in the morning."

   This paragraph really says:

   _____ a) He wants to work.

   _____ b) He doesn't want to work.

   _____ c) She thinks her brother is important.

Understanding the Meaning

What does it really mean?

When you are writing a composition, you may want to give your opinion. Sometimes you want other people to agree with you. Usually the best way to get people to agree with your opinion is to give a good example of what you believe. Here is part of George's composition on A Good Job.

> A good job is always interesting to the worker. Sometimes people think that a good job pays a lot of money. I don't think that is necessarily true. A teacher doesn't always earn a lot of money, but many teachers like the work because it is interesting and satisfying.

In this composition George has given his opinion. He also gives an example (teaching) to show that his opinion is correct.

Many times writers do not say what their opinions are. You can tell what they think, however, by the examples they give. Here is an example:

> Everyone was laughing. John's face became redder and redder. "I didn't mean to say that," he said. He looked at the smiles on everyone's face and thought, Can these be my friends?

In this paragraph, do you think the writer is telling us that John's friends like him? Not really. The writer shows us his opinion with the word "laughing" and John's silent question, "Can these be my friends?"

Always look for the meaning behind the words.

What does it really mean?

Decide which meaning is correct for these paragraphs.
Write an X next to your choice.

1. We sat in the living room, and Ellen kept smiling and smiling. No one said anything. "There's a beautiful birthday cake for later," Ellen told us. "Isn't this fun?" I looked at my friend Tex, and he looked at me. We didn't answer her.

The writer's opinion is:

_____ a) That the party wasn't much fun.

_____ b) That the party was fun.

_____ c) That Tex liked the party.

2. The foreman said, "Men, I don't want you to work hard. We're only behind in our work five days because the machine broke down. The company doesn't need the money they lost. We don't need the money either. Let's take it easy today. Who cares how long the unemployment lines are?"

The writer wants us to understand:

_____ a) That the foreman thinks the men shouldn't work hard.

_____ b) That the company is rich.

_____ c) That the foreman thinks the men should work hard.

3. Sara looked into the store window. Inside there were beautiful warm coats. Outside in the cold, she put her hand in her pocket and touched her wallet. "I don't really need a coat yet," she said to herself.

The writer wants us to know:

_____ a) That Sara is going into the store.

_____ b) That Sara doesn't need a coat.

_____ c) That Sara needs a coat.

4. After dinner I was listening to my favorite rock group. My father came in the room and shouted, "Why don't you turn the radio louder? I can't hear it very well."

The writer wants us to understand:
_____ a) That the music wasn't loud enough.

_____ b) That his father was really telling him that the music was too loud.

_____ c) That his father loves rock music.

Reading about Emotions

How do you recognize mood?

When you read stories, you can understand them better if you can recognize moods or emotions. Authors do not always tell you the words for the emotions. They show the emotions of their characters through their actions.

Here is an example of an author showing that someone is angry:

> She walked around and around the room. She couldn't sit down. Her mouth was a straight line, and her eyes looked like fire. She kept opening and closing her hands and talking to herself.

Nowhere does the author say that the woman is angry. You understand that she is through her actions.

Here is an example of an author showing that someone is happy:

> He couldn't stop smiling as he walked down the street. He smiled at everyone and everything. "Hello," he said to the bus driver. "Isn't it a great day?"

Again you do not read the word happy, but you understand that the man is happy by the way he behaves.

These are the words for some important emotions.

sad — not happy
proud — being pleased with oneself
ashamed — not proud
greedy — wanting everything for oneself

How do you recognize mood?

A Decide which emotion the speaker is showing. Put the
letter of the emotion on the line.

a) sad   b) ashamed   c) proud   d) greedy   e) happy

1. I didn't want to look at him. Now he knew exactly what
   I had done. I wished that yesterday could be lived all
   over again.   _____

2. Our family is very important. Many of us have been
   famous. We are well known throughout our country.   _____

3. I didn't want to watch her. How could she sit there and
   eat all of the cake and not give me more than one piece?   _____

4. After I read the letter, I sat down beside the window
   and looked out. There were children playing, people
   laughing, and the sky was blue. No one could
   understand how I felt.   _____

5. My heart was singing. I won first prize in the Science
   Fair.   _____

B Read the paragraphs and then the questions. Choose the
correct answer and write the letter on the line.

> "I'm sorry," I said. The teacher looked at me. "You
> should be sorry," she said, "I always thought you were my
> best student." I felt my head go down on the desk, and the
> tears began.

1. I feel   a) happy.   b) angry.   c) ashamed.   _____

2. My teacher is   a) proud.   b) happy.   c) sad.   _____

Facts in Advertising

What can you believe in advertising?

When you read an advertisement in the newspaper or watch
a commercial on television, you must be able to decide
what is fact and what is opinion. The people who advertise
want you to buy their product. They will say many nice
things about their product for that reason. Look and listen
carefully to understand what is fact and what is not.

Here is an example:

> Come to Florida where all your dreams will come true.
> Swim in the warm Gulf or the exciting Atlantic. Play golf
> on championship golf courses. Dine at the best restaurants.
> Dance until morning at fun discos. You'll have the vacation
> of a lifetime in Florida.

When you see an ad like this, begin to ask yourself
questions. Will all your dreams come true if you go to
Florida? Is it probable that you will have the vacation of a
lifetime there? The ad has some facts about swimming,
playing golf, eating and dancing. Some things, however, are
not necessarily facts but opinion.

Learn to recognize opinion when you read newspapers
and watch television. Remember, ads say good things about
the product because the advertiser wants you to buy it.
Some things may be true, but some are just opinion.

What can you believe in advertising?

A   Read this advertisement. Then answer the questions.

> GENUINE DIAMOND EARRINGS
> FOR JUST $5.00
> Have you always wanted diamonds? Here's your
> chance to own them at an incredibly low price.
> Friends will admire them. Others will envy you.
> This special offer is only for the readers of this
> newspaper, for a limited time only. Send your five
> dollar check or money order today!

1. Does the ad say how large the earrings are?   Yes _____   No _____

2. Are some diamonds better than others?   Yes _____   No _____

3. Will your friends admire you more when you have diamonds?   Yes _____   No _____

4. Do you think this is really a special?   Yes _____   No _____

5. Do you think this ad is only in this newspaper?   Yes _____   No _____

6. Is this probably a good bargain?   Yes _____   No _____

B   Read this advertisement for television. Then answer the questions.

> ANNOUNCER: Whiter than white! Brighter than bright! Those are your teeth
> when you use Happy Toothpaste. People will love your smile. You'll love
> your looks. Buy Happy Toothpaste at your drugstore today.

1. Is any color whiter than white?   Yes _____   No _____

2. Is there anything brighter than bright?   Yes _____   No _____

3. Do people "love" brighter smiles?   Yes _____   No _____

4. Will Happy Toothpaste make you happy?   Yes _____   No _____

5. Will clean teeth make you "love" your looks?   Yes _____   No _____

6. Can a toothpaste change the way you look?   Yes _____   No _____

The Language of Algebra

What are special Algebra words?

Algebra is a kind of Math that has its own vocabulary.
When you take Algebra, you will use regular Math
words like

add $(+)$ subtract $(-)$ multiply $(\times)$ divide $(\div)$

but you also need to know other words and phrases. Here
is some of that new vocabulary.

numeral   means   a number. Sometimes it is also called a constant.

variable   means   something that represents any number.

Examples: 5, 6, 7, 8   are numerals

b, X, b_1, $\triangle$ are variables

A numerical phrase or expression is   one or more numbers with or
without symbols like $\div$, $<$, $+$

An algebraic phrase or expression is   one or more numbers or variables
with or without symbols like
$=$, $\div$, $\sqrt{}$

Examples: 18, 5^6, $10 + 6$, 11×8 are numerical phrases

$a + b$, $a - 10x$, $\sqrt{5y^2 \div 9}$ are algebraic phrases

It is important to know also that in an algebraic
expression it is not necessary to use the symbol $\times$ for
multiplication when there is a variable in the expression.
This means

5×10 is correct, but $5 \times a$ is not. It should be $5a$.

What are special Algebra words?

A   Put a check in front of the correct answer:

1. 112   is a   ____ numeral   ____ variable

2. c   is a   ____ numeral   ____ variable

3. 9 − 8   is a   ____ numerical phrase   ____ algebraic phrase

4. a − 3   is a   ____ numerical phrase   ____ algebraic phrase

5. 6 × y   is   ____ correct   ____ not correct

6. 27b   is   ____ correct   ____ not correct

7. △   is a   ____ numeral   ____ variable

8. x   is a   ____ numeral   ____ variable

B   Complete the sentences with one of the vocabulary
words or phrases below.

1. Something that represents any number is a _____.

2. One or more numbers or variables with or without symbols is a(n)

   _____.

3. One or more numbers with or without symbols is a(n) _____.

4. A number is also called a(n) _____.

5. In an algebraic expression it is not necessary to use _____.

algebraic expression	numeral	the symbol ×
numerical expression	variable	

C   Memorize the definitions of numeral, constant, variable,
numerical phrase and algebraic phrase.

Science Experiments

What are some special Science experiment words?

In Science many times you need to know special vocabulary
for the tests or experiments that you do. Here are some
words that will help you.

This is a Bunsen burner.

This is a test tube.

This is a petri dish.

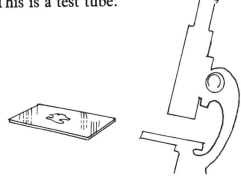

This is a slide.

This is a solution. It is liquid. It includes
something other than water.

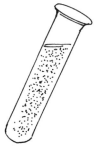

This is an emulsion. It is thick and usually
looks like milk.

A stain is a color that is used on a slide in an experiment.
Sterile means something that is medically clean.

What are some special Science experiment words?

A Choose the correct word(s) and write it on the line.

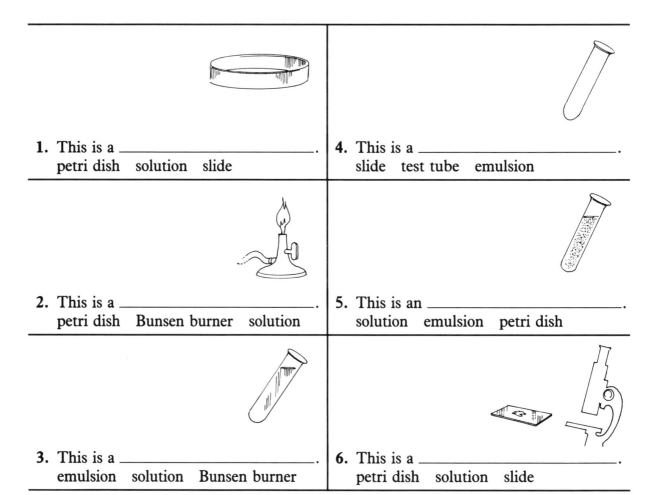

1. This is a _____.
   petri dish   solution   slide

2. This is a _____.
   petri dish   Bunsen burner   solution

3. This is a _____.
   emulsion   solution   Bunsen burner

4. This is a _____.
   slide   test tube   emulsion

5. This is an _____.
   solution   emulsion   petri dish

6. This is a _____.
   petri dish   solution   slide

B Write the correct word(s) on the line.

1. _____
2. _____
3. _____
4. _____

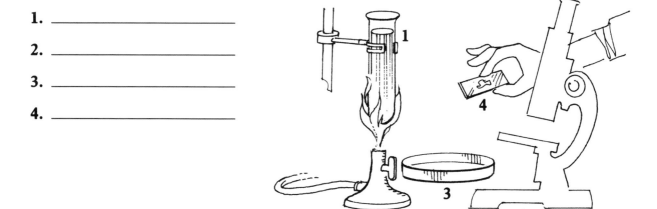

Special Computer Vocabulary

What are some special Computer words?

There are many words that have special meanings when we are talking about computers.

      menu   cursor   mouse   function   pen

A menu is a list of food in a restaurant. With computers a menu is a list of information we can ask the computer about.

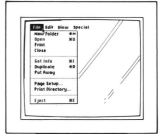

When we tell a computer which direction to move, a light on the screen shows where the next symbol will be printed. This is called a cursor.

A mouse is a small animal. With computers, a mouse is a box with buttons that we use to tell the cursor in which direction to move.

A function means a use of something. Some computers have function keys that we use to tell the computer to do a specific function.

We use a keyboard to talk to the computer. With some computers we can talk to the computer on the screen, using a special pen.

What are some special Computer words?

A Choose the correct word(s) and write it on the line.

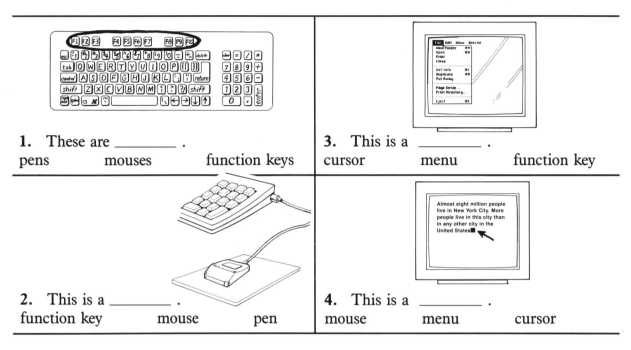

1. These are _____ .
pens   mouses   function keys

3. This is a _____ .
cursor   menu   function key

2. This is a _____ .
function key   mouse   pen

4. This is a _____ .
mouse   menu   cursor

B Write the correct word(s) on the line.

1. _____

2. _____

3. _____

4. _____

5. _____

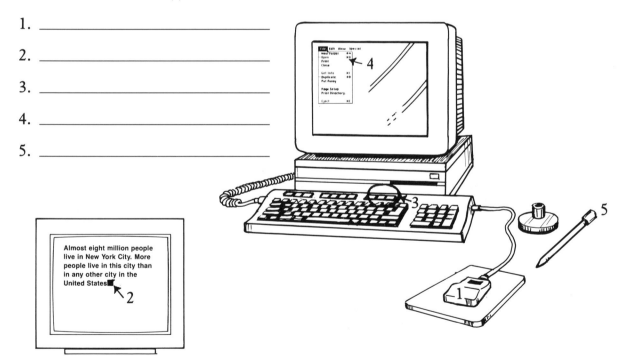

Almost eight million people
live in New York City. More
people live in this city than
in any other city in the
United States

Special Computer Vocabulary

What are some special Computer words?

You know some words to use in talking about computers. Here are more.

| data | input | output | graphics | prompt | modem |

The computer is a machine. It needs information to operate.
Information the computer uses is called <u>data</u>.

Information or data that we give the computer is <u>input</u>.
Data that the computer gives us is <u>output</u>.

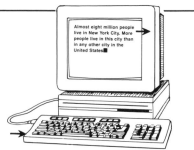

The computer uses words or letters and pictures.
The pictures on a computer are called <u>graphics</u>.

Sometimes after input, the computer wants to ask a
question. This question is sometimes indicated by a symbol
on the screen called a <u>prompt</u>.

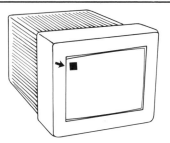

A computer can talk to other computers. It does this with a
telephone line and a special machine called a <u>modem</u>.

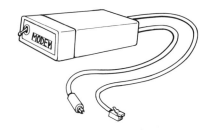

What are some special Computer words?

A Choose the correct word and write it on the line.

1. This is _____ .
modem   prompt   data

4. This is a _____ .
graphic   modem   cursor

2. This is a _____ .
input   prompt   output

5. This is _____ .
input   modem   cursor

3. This is _____ .
cursor   data   output

6. These are _____ .
graphics   modems   prompts

B Write the correct word(s) on the line.

1. _____

2. _____

3. _____

4. _____

5. _____

6. _____

1

2

3

4

5

6

Special Meanings

How do you understand special phrases?

Sometimes when you read there are phrases or groups of words that have a special meaning. They do not mean exactly what they say. Here is an example:

>She eats like a bird.

This woman does not eat the same thing as a bird. She does not eat her food without hands like a bird, either. The phrase "eats like a bird" really means that she does not eat very much.

Here is another example:

>From the mountain I could see to the ends of the world.

Where is the end of the world? How could you see it from the top of a mountain? The phrase "see to the ends of the world" really means to see a long distance.

The English language has many phrases like these. When you are reading, you will find them often. Poetry has such phrases. Here are some examples you might find in poems:

>The road was silver under the moon.
>
>Eyes like deep pools of water.
>
>The smiling waters of the river.

The road was not silver, of course. The eyes were not deep pools, and the river water could not smile. When we read language like this, we understand that the author is giving us a special idea or making us feel a special emotion.

How do you understand special phrases?

A Many special meanings are comparisons. Read the
phrases below and then select the best word to
complete them:

1. The child was as ____ as a mouse.
   a) new   b) busy   c) quiet

   _____

2. My daughter Susie can run as fast as the ____.
   a) clock   b) wind   c) washing machine

   _____

3. I'm so sad that I could cry a ____.
   a) river   b) water   c) glass

   _____

4. "You're as pretty as a ____," he said.
   a) house   b) flower   c) vegetable

   _____

5. The sky was as black as ____.
   a) coal   b) day   c) a pencil

   _____

6. The skyscraper was as tall as a ____.
   a) company   b) mountain   c) school

   _____

7. He was so ill that he was as white as a ____.
   a) window   b) piece of paper   c) doctor

   _____

8. The crashing noise was as loud as ____.
   a) my radio   b) thunder   c) a bell

   _____

B Learn to look for special meaning phrases. Read these,
decide what they mean and put the letter of the correct
meaning on the line.

1. "As tall as a tree" means
   a) ten feet tall.   b) very tall.   c) twenty feet tall.   _____

2. "As heavy as a lead balloon" means
   a) very heavy.   b) very light.   c) yellow and gold.   _____

3. "Walking on air" means
   a) stepping in the air.   b) flying.   c) walking happily. _____

4. "Soft as a cat" means
   a) made of cat fur.   b) very soft.   c) very hard.   _____

5. "As free as a bird" means
   a) able to fly.   b) very small.   c) very free.   _____

6. "As hot as a stove" means
   a) not very hot.   b) very hot.   c) very cold.   _____

7. "As pretty as a picture" means
   a) very pretty.   b) ugly.   c) very short.   _____

8. "As sick as a dog" means
   a) well.   b) sick.   c) like a dog.   _____

Special Meanings

How do you understand special phrases?

When you read phrases with special meanings, sometimes you do not understand because they are jokes. There are jokes in most languages. Some jokes take something impossible and make it funny.

Here is an example of special meanings through jokes (humor):

> It was so cold that the fire froze in the fireplace.

Does fire freeze? Of course not. The author is using this impossible happening to tell us that it was very cold, and to tell us with humor.

> My father was so old that he really was his own grandfather.

Is that possible? Can you be your own grandfather? No, but it makes us understand in a humorous way that the man was old.

Here are some more examples:

> The plane flew so fast it arrived five minutes before it left.
> It was so high it took two men to climb it.
> The man told so many tall stories (lies) that he grew two inches.
> She was so mean it took five pounds of sugar to sweeten her tea.
> We ate leftovers for two years and five months after the party.
> Her feet were so long that they didn't stop till Tuesday.

Many times it is hard to understand what other people think is funny. Humor does come from the impossible many times. Many special meaning phrases are humorous because they are impossible.

How do you understand special phrases?

A Finish each phrase to make it humorous:

1. As tall as _____

2. As silly as _____

3. As hot as _____

4. As tired as _____

5. As rich as _____

6. As delicious as _____

7. As clean as _____

8. As heavy as _____

B Finish each sentence with a phrase that you think is humorous.

1. He said, "I love you very much. You are _____

_____."

2. What did the chicken say when it saw the farmer? "_____

_____."

3. Sit down and relax. You must be _____

_____.

4. The waiter told the cook, "A man ate the soup just now

and said it was _____."

5. The secretary said, "My boss' husband is so tall that _____

_____."

6. That man is so rich that he _____

_____.